FAR F

Born in Johnstone in 1963, Jim Carruth grew up on his family's farm in Renfrewshire. His first collection *Bovine Pastoral* (2004) was the first of a sequence of five chapbooks that captured the experiences of those working in the rural landscape. His work has attracted both praise and awards, including the McLellan Poetry Competition, the McCash Poetry Prize and the Callum Macdonald Memorial Award. In 2009, he was awarded a Robert Louis Stevenson Fellowship. He has collaborated with sculptor Andy Scott on several projects over the years, most notably *The Kelpies*, and in 2014, he was appointed as the Poet Laureate for Glasgow. In 2015, his verse novella *Killochries* was shortlisted for the Saltire Society Scottish Poetry Book of the Year, the Seamus Heaney Centre for Poetry Prize and the Fenton Aldeburgh Prize. *Far Field* is the final part of *The Auchensale Trilogy* following on from *Black Cart* (2017) and *Bale Fire* (2019).

'*Far Field* is the stunning culmination of a hugely ambitious trilogy celebrating Carruth's love for a rural landscape and its people. In essence, think of *A Scots Quair* as enduring song. I cannot think of any other collection which so intimately and sensitively documents a beloved corner of a beloved country and the folk who farmed there, through all their seasons and weathers.'

JOHN GLENDAY

'In deeply moving poems, as fierce as they are tender, Carruth honours a way of life that is threatened or already lost. His vivid language immerses us in the daily work of caring for animals, fields, family and neighbours. Every line is as honed as the landscape, evoking the harrowing, relentless aspects of farming as well as the meaning and beauty to be found in everyday routines. Endurance is threaded through the collection as is love and the potential for regeneration.'

JANE CLARKE

'*Far Field* completes Jim Carruth's marvellous trilogy that began with *Black Cart* and *Bale Fire*. I am in awe of his verbal power and the author's fidelity to love, loss, and community. This is a book of land and landscapes, and the gift of being alive to them.'

DAVID MORLEY

FAR FIELD

Jim Carruth

Jim Carruth
Glasgow 2023

Polygon

First published in paperback in Great Britain in 2023 by
Polygon, an imprint of Birlinn Ltd.

Birlinn Ltd
West Newington House
10 Newington Road
Edinburgh EH9 1QS

www.polygonbooks.co.uk

ISBN 978 1 84697 636 0
EBOOK ISBN 978 1 78885 578 5

British Library Cataloguing-in-Publication Data
A catalogue record for this book is available on
request from the British Library.

The publisher gratefully acknowledges investment from
Creative Scotland towards the publication of this book.

Typeset in Verdigris MVB by The Foundry, Edinburgh
Printed and bound in Great Britain by Clays Ltd, Elcograf S.p.A.

For Lorna, David, Hannah and Paul

CONTENTS

2. EARTHSTRUCK

3. STEPPING STONES

The footers in the first section trace a journey across the body of a cow. The footers in the second section are the main buildings in the family farm providing the physical definition of home. The footers in the final section are the many different spellings of the family name. As many of the descendants in the past were illiterate farm workers this has led to the variety seen today.

A number of poems in the first part of the book have been inspired by the work of the Glasgow Boys in the late nineteenth century. Early in their careers, some of the artists focussed on working 'en plein air' within rural communities trying to capture a more naturalistic response to those who worked there. The following works have been used as starting points to poems in the collection:

Landscape with Cattle	Joseph Crawhall
A Hind's Daughter	James Guthrie
Boy with a Straw	James Guthrie
Schoolmates	James Guthrie
The Milkmaid	George Henry
Sheep Shearing	James Guthrie
The Hedgecutter	George Henry
Gypsy Fires are Burning for	
Daylight's Past and Gone	James Guthrie
The Gamekeeper's Daughter	E.A. Walton

'Playing the Milkmaid in the Hameau de la Reine': Marie Antionette used to amuse herself and her friends by portraying a milkmaid in her own rustic landscape created by architect Richard Mique.

'Four millimetres' describes the regular TB testing of cattle.

'My Wife's Whistle': Wellees is the name of my brother-in-law's farm.

gifts

from my father
the lyric rhythm
of furrow

from my mother
the fertile depth
of soil

LANDSCAPE WITH

CATTLE

Okay, I like cows

GEORGE BAILEY

Landscape with Cattle

On these flooded flatlands perspective is key
as is the journey my eye has taken
from the distant horizon set by the sea.

Its ripple seen in the middle distance
in the ridge line of the red-roofed cottage
and in the foreground's straight-backed cattle.

These white beasts have grown to fill my view.
Standing in shallow water, offering up reflections,
I find the deep calm of their cud chewing

cannot easily be conveyed, nor its stark contrast
with a day's busyness: flit and twist of swallows
circling at their necks, across their strong bodies.

Each feathered flight a first stroke on the canvas
the artist takes then removes, time and again
struggling with the scale of the task in hand.

A Hind's Daughter

Left on this canvas: ragged dark fringe,
earth skin, clothed in rough hand-me-downs
caught in an everyday chore – forever a scowl.

I was chosen for this task, one from eight
to stand for hours through an east wind chill;
one hand frozen to the handle of blade glint

the other holding the ribbed cabbage stalk
for nothing but his mother's bread and milk
and this painting that does not show me true.

Straw

Boy with a straw
from the stook

in his mouth
sitting idle

and chewing
on a thought.

There are times
when this world

is to be gazed on
and tasted.

By Heart

Not a childhood scarred
by multiplication tables

that forced march
through growing numbers

confused progress
chanted out in unison

nor those trials of
memorising archaic verse

stumbling over words
at the front of the class

but the passion to recall
all that is important:

field, hedge, fence, farm
words linked together

a mnemonic web
to capture home.

Schoolmates

The longest walks were the ones trudged
through early years and winter months
the worst of all weathers in heavy boots,
working clothes more suited for the field,
slow miles from farmyard to the iron gates
to arrive late behind the calling of the bell.
There to learn from the discipline of the strap
that when words are clumsy on the tongue
and your rough hands have struggled all day
to line them up in the right order on the page
while all around you, pupils wield laughter
as a weapon, best choose a hunter's silence.

Barefoot Days

My barefoot days would always end like this –
my mother's call to have me come back in.
Because real love is rarely hug and kiss,
she would lift me on to the kitchen sink.
Head bowed to the task in active prayer,
she'd work the dirty soles of her firstborn,
thumbs together, teasing out sharp thorns,
scrubbing away the day's dirt in layers.

First the afternoon, racing in the fields;
underneath, the morning, bales in the byre.
The start of the journey slowly revealed
in small white legs drying by the fire.
Her cleansing – absolution and permission
that come tomorrow, I could start again.

Milk Tank

Errand set, I was tasked to fulfil a mother's request
but first placed my hand on the side of the tank

felt the tremor of an ocean churn, the power
of the swell as the big paddle strained to turn

and chill the load and heat of mothers' milk
trapped inside this shine of stainless steel.

A minor deity, I'd struggle with the heavy lid to gaze
on thick cream frothing in the well of Parnassus;

scooped out our small share before the lorry
with its thirsty pipe sucked up all its treasure.

Its engine changed tone when it drew in air
as milk shallowed to the trickle of a summer burn.

Something ungrateful with the way this was taken.
Did it not know each drop should be savoured

that drinking maintained the bond,
kept me a child of the herd?

The Basics

Putting on and milking out

To clean the udder
warm damp cloth
doused in the bucket

To draw from four teats,
checking for mastitis thickness
encourage the flow

To attach each cluster's cup
till it clings on and sucks
to the rhythm of the pump

To move on up the line

Taking off and sending out

To check the vessel's empty
To flick off the catch
remove the cluster

To dip it in the disinfectant pail
hang it on the hook
spray each teat

To release the catch on the gate
to slap their rears
send the mothers out

To let the next lot in

Putting on and milking out
Taking off and sending out
Let the next lot in

Playing the Milkmaid in the Hameau de la Reine

The difference between those who treat this
as a pretence, a dressing up, a rural escape
never as a regular chore essential for living
and the manner of the experienced herdsman
is that common touch, a hard-won empathy.

Too much talk distracts you from the animal
as does your laughter at the drizzle of milk
and with your face too close to the bucket
you cannot see the signs, sense its tremor
a growing unrest in the gestures of the tail

so miss the changing moods of the beast
unhappy with its chains, the daily demands
of servitude, unsettled, shifting its weight
from one back leg to another, readying itself.
One swift kick and you could lose your head.

Flow

How did a world thirsty for signs
miss, during this winter's heavy fall,

the farm road blocked for days
the lorry that could not lift our milk

the cows that could not stop their flow
and that task any dairyman dreads

taking the heavy plug out of the tank
releasing the milk into the ground.

Those not there to witness our loss
possibly picture this as white on white.

Not so – it was yellowed cream
seeping through dirt-flecked snow.

Trawlerman

His waterproofs weighing heavy as sin
are meant for severe weather – the worst
that can be thrown at you on rough seas

but here he stands, safe enough on dry land
where the most he can expect to receive
is a short spurt of a shower on a sunny day.

Still, he has the haunted look of Captain Ahab
standing dwarfed by such a large mammal
fear drowned out by its rutting walrus bellow.

As it swells up before him to mount the cow
he must slip the semen sheath on underneath –
today's brief catch the beginning of life.

Anatomical Model of the Cow

(Vinton's Livestock Models No. 4   Price 2/6 Net)

Peeling back each layer of nature's building blocks
I move beyond the outward confirmation of cow
that names all that can be seen from nose to tail,
shoulder to hoof and soon I face the skeleton:
this grand architecture of head, trunk and limbs.
I repeat the words: lunar, magnum, scaphoid
then explore the pumping life of arteries and veins
before turning to the muscles in all their Latin glory.
At last, I'm left to unpick the mystery of soft organs.
Folding back the lung, reveals the heart beneath.
Bending round the left half of the diaphragm
leads me to the first stomach and the spleen.
Turn right and the other three stomachs appear.
This journey continues with the mesentery
jejunum, colon and rectum which I lift up
for the final surprise: hidden away for safety
a healthy calf sheltered in the centre of it all.

Days of Whitewash
(for Babs)

The days of whitewash were all too rare.
Late in the season, they required many hands.
This was a job for all the family and only started
when the more important ones were done.

Cleaning the wall first of cobwebs and dirt
my father then took a strong wooden stick
to mix and thicken in knee-high buckets
his thin porridge of powder and water.

We started on the ground then up high ladders.
Our slosh of long brushes – a grateful offering to
this old farmhouse god who'd put a roof over us,
kept us warm and dry through winter storms.

After the house came loose box, barn, byre.
This was a serving up of the dripping feast.
Adults, children, dogs, windows, all splattered
in a celebration both exuberant and messy.

Touched by the joy of this summer rain
we were the speckled offspring of the farm
covering up a harsher past with Sunday best;
our eyes wide open, dazzled, snow-blind.

Shearing

Sweat and technique to hold tight
a bad-tempered blackie
turned on its back, its head on your hip,
its feet off the ground.

Feeling the weight and heft of it
struggle with the wriggle and butt of it;
careful not to nick and bleed;
the arc of the clipper underneath.

Sweep follows graceful sweep
ripples out across the belly, around the legs
along the flank, over the shoulder,
until, with a buzzing in its ear, it is over.

Scythe

Each summer break I was sent to clear fields;
a growing up and into the curves of the scythe.
The technique at first rusty but soon remembered
in the arch of my tight spine, the arc of the blade
sharpened by my dad each morning to wink at the sun.
On the long curve and bevel of its wooden snath
a firm grip, left above right, on fist-thick handles
to lift above my shoulders, sweep and follow through
leaving bean weeds, thistles, nettles flat on their back;
the taunts of purple and yellow heads a memory.
Walking for miles on retribution, callouses forming,
till my anger subsided and I was at one with the task
for I'd mastered the rhythm of a man-made breeze.

The Hedgecutter

In the landscape of hill criss-crossed by dyke
and fence, where desire for straight borders
is a telling of our story as order and control,
his way is a slicing and stripping back of nature
a reigning in, a shaping, a seeking of symmetry.

Without lifting his head to a skyline's clues,
those untamed silhouettes of oak and beech,
he hacks the tough tendrils of blackthorn
though they will soon blunt his blades.

Decades have stiffened his neck, bent
his spine to the hedge, wearied the wrist.

Who cares? Come next year
spring will set out again
with defiant bud and branch
in a myriad of glorious directions.

Days Left Till Harvest

Because the world did not hunger
for his word nor seek him out,
this man of whispered wisdom and silence,

I cherish these moments in his company –
standing at the edge of the wheat
working out the days left till harvest

when the wind picked up from the west
and in front of us as one great wave,
the ears of the field turned to him.

Harvest Epilogue

After all that effort of harvesting
this one field from last year's ploughing,
tortuous, slow, hours bogged down
in the clutch of heavy clay until that final rush
with the big combine to claim the barley
in a break in the weather, not finishing
the final row till well after midnight –
that coupling and decoupling of lights
on the hill, strange to find the big bales
lying there unsheltered through the worst
of winter, left untouched, discarded
their future worth an unanswered question.

Harvest Wake

Damp and dusk huddle
round dying flames

old summer smothered
in a smoke of slow heat –

leaves, blackthorn branches
smoulder by empty fields.

Muffled voices splutter,
curse the year's turning.

From tongues lost to song –
silence demands its time.

Shrunk indistinct figures
truckled in mud

stare beyond embers –
distance in expressions lit.

Journey in the hung head
of a hobbled cob,

in the white of its long face
the road ahead.

Gypsy fires are burning
for daylight's past and gone.

The Hireling's Lullaby

If your song is such a lullaby
why does the baby on the teat still cry?

How can there be so much distress
when suckled by a mother's breast?

In the byre, our cattle roar in pain
at the merest snatch of your refrain

the sky has turned a different light
and none of us will sleep this night.

That song you've sung for hours and hours
has soured milk and wilted flowers;

set brothers at each other's throats
with the fury of a sack of stoats.

The very sound of your strange lilt
flattened dykes our fathers built.

Even the beams of solid stead
creak and rage above our heads.

This wretched night could be no worse
had we lived out some tinker's curse.

If your song is such a lullaby
why does the baby on the teat still cry?

EARTHSTRUCK

Ploughmen have ploughed my back and made their furrows long
Psalm 129:3

Earthstruck

The neighbour's son, whose words
were a stumble on rough ground,

whose cack-handedness at simple chores
drew the anger of his father's fists,

once watched her all day over the dyke
ploughing that one field set for barley.

Becoming used to his stare, she turned
her own gaze back to the depth of soil

before bedrock, that one boggy corner,
the tricky curves and angles of slopes

but would catch his stooped silhouette,
his head's ragged hedge fenced in

by her wing mirrors, as she swung
the tractor around at the headland.

He stood at the edge of his known world –
followed her from the dropping of the blade

for her first furrow till in failing light
the lifting of it for the last time,

speechless at each line drawn on the land:
straight, uninterrupted, confident, true.

A Rough Sonnet from the Blacksmith's Son

Mine is not a life to be talked about
by your village teacher, his weak mouth
quoting instead from an old book's musty page
whose every sentence lacks a living breath.

But bring your lame mare into my dim light
and I will show by the forge's bright flame
a lesson worked from strain and coursing sweat
this muscle sculpting of my whole frame.

I am the tender shape, and bend, the sight,
the heat, a rhythmic hammer's clanging beat
ringing out to find each shoe's perfect fit.
My dousing water cools the molten heat.

My power is the ploughshare and the sword
a life and death punched out in every word.

The Gamekeeper's Daughter

'This fictional account of the day-to-day life of an English game-keeper is of considerable interest to outdoor minded readers, as it contains many passages on pheasant raising, the apprehending of poachers, ways to control vermin, and other chores and duties of the professional gamekeeper. Unfortunately, one is obliged to wade through many pages of extraneous material.'

Review of *Lady Chatterley's Lover*
in *Field and Stream*, November 1959

As hounds yelp distant on the moor
he will use his poacher's map,
tip toeing past traps in the wood

to reach an unlocked cottage door.
The coat hooks are empty, boots gone
but he smells her father everywhere.

Still the lure is great, she calls
and he follows, undressing fast
like the thrashing of a salmon.

He slips in closer to his singing prey.
Her body lies still, skin soft as fawn;
her song is of the trapped and sprung.

The way she raises her eyebrow
with the gentle lifting of the latch
is the look of hunter not hunted.

Tenderness

i. Hugo is Tender

was the phrase uttered at dinner by the youngest
as she sat with three generations at the table
eating their evening meal of generous portions.
Just a guest, I was struck by the teenager's words
the openness, that sharing of a close confidence.
I pictured then, his holding and cradling of her
a soft caress of rough hands at the end of the day
and all those gathered there even her granddad
could sense it too, nodding knowingly as one
and accepted it in that safe space where later
one other family secret would reveal itself –
that for the last eight years on this hill farm
the pet lambs had been named alphabetically.

ii. The Pig Whisperer

Less well known the work of the pig whisperer
who sidles in alongside the sow in the crowded sty
to fill the wide whorl of her ear with fancy words.
In this squalor and stench he soothes the troubled beast
with hope of a future filled with sun-kissed pasture.
She doesn't get language, so the sense is redundant
but like a baby in a cradle his lullaby pentameter,
silky assonance and deep smooth voice calms her,
slowing her fast heartbeat, relaxing her large frame.
She wallows in the wonderful lies of a happy life,
those expensive cuts rippling on her hind quarters.
Each promise she savours in her ear now
he'll also savour later, sweet on his own tongue.

You Smell of the Farm

'How could some yokel cast a spell on your heart?' – Sappho

In what way? Enlighten me. Come on, try
to put some detail to your broadside sneer.
Is it something of the beasts that have rubbed
off on me – their hide, their hair, their breath?
Do not mince your words – is it their shit?

I've handled dry matted dung, waded shin-deep
as slurry sloshed over my wellies. Is your sense
of smell sensitive to the seasons, maybe to a whiff
of barley chaff, the stench of silage or stale sweat,
of physical work ingrained, marking me like a tattoo?

Is smell the only sense you wish to utilise for this
branding? Do I sound of the farm for example?
Do I have the look of the farm? Come closer –
see deep grooved into my palms are mud, blood.
Take your hand in mine, touch the living and dead.

At First Sight

Years later you'd own up
that 'at first sight' was a half-truth

our chance encounter
at the barn dance pre-planned

your reluctant friend
tasked to distract my brother
while you made the move.

What attracted you
to me was that I was not,
repeat not, the finished article

but presented you an opportunity
to work dull clay till harvest

allied to my undoubted willingness
to offer up my future seasons,
a real commitment to the cause,

one who despite an allergy to straw
sat on a bale for hours with you
patiently waiting for our first kiss.

A Good Judge of Horse Flesh

The way she cast an eye over the animal that day
out in the yard as the dishevelled stable boy held on
inspecting everything from the character of the head
to its long neck, shoulder, strong back, depth of girth
checking the balance was true, the muscling and tone
careful to make the right decision, for one mistake
in choosing a stallion for stud marks the offspring.
Moving closer, she'd feel the strength in each leg
the soundness of the feet, the condition of its coat.
That patient way she viewed the horse from all angles
from side and back, first at rest and then to and fro
across the cobbles – the walk, the jog, and the trot
was the way at the dancing she once looked at me.

Missing the Harvest Dance

Where have you been
this year's harvest queen
with your tousled hair
and your devil-may-care?

Where have you been
this year's harvest queen
with your tousled hair
and your devil-may-care
and your winner's sash
with its torn tartan flash?

Where have you been
this year's harvest queen
with your tousled hair
and your devil-may-care
and your winner's sash
with its torn tartan flash
and your one patent shoe
and your crown lost too?

Where have you been
this year's harvest queen
with your tousled hair
and your devil-may-care
and your winner's sash
with its torn tartan flash
and your one patent shoe
and your crown lost too
and your crumpled dress
and your mother's distress?

Where have you been
this year's harvest queen
with your tousled hair
and your devil-may-care
and your winner's sash
with its torn tartan flash
and your one patent shoe
and your crown lost too
and your crumpled dress
and your mother's distress
at the huntsman's grin
that followed you in?

Where have you been
my harvest queen?

Leviathan

First witness this warm August night
a son and daughter of the soil,
lovers on a floor of loose straw.

Remnants of the harvest
stripped bare, sharing each other
they defy the signs by lying together

in the belly of an old tithe barn,
its carcass picked clean to its ribs.
This great beast has lost its song.

It will not swallow another year.
Above this land, seeds spilled
across the sky are dying lights.

Prophet, take this portent to Nineveh:
that humming glow on the horizon.
Forget nothing on your journey.

Every Man his Own Cattle Doctor

(a practical treatise on the diseases of horned cattle, and sheep by
Francis Clater first published in 1810)

The all-wise disposer of events has thought it good
to reduce all the animal creation
under the power and dominion of man.

Neat Cattle in particular may be said to rank
the foremost in the creation,
especially when we consider their great utility,
and the wonderful variety of productions
these valuable animals afford towards
the support and use of mankind.

Horned Cattle, particularly Cows, are subject to
a great variety of diseases,
which are for the most part brought on
by the different effects of the elements
on the animal frame,
and often in a few days reduce them
from the greatest state of perfection
to a mere skeleton.

i. Black-leg, quarter-evil, or black quarter

*This disease is called by a great number of other names; all
indicate the same disorder.*

*The quarter-evil chiefly affects, such as they are, in the best
condition, young cattle from one or two years old when the
vegetable creation springs up in all its perfection, the young
animals are not able to stand against such luxurious living.*

Days when the words swell up within you.
Such a glut after winter's meagre pickings
you cannot find release.

Take twelve white poppy heads
one hand-full of freshly gathered wormwood
and marshmallow roots.

Bruise the poppy heads,
slice the wormwood and roots
boil them in two gallons of ale dregs.

Then take two or three large pieces of flannel,
and wring them out of the liquor as hot as you can,
and apply them to the growth.

A poultice draws up vowels from a deep well.
The swollen blister of a sentence when ready,
must be lanced by a proper knife picked for the purpose.

ii. Staggers, vertigo or swimming in the head

This disease mostly attacks animals that have been kept in a state of poverty and starvation during the winter season; and which have in the spring of the year been admitted into fertile pasture.

It is the going without
when teenage weeks are like years
frustration surrounded by over activity.

Did you recognise that hunger
in my eyes that night at the barn dance
when you picked me up?

Swimming in the head still
after all these years,
I do not seek a cure.

iii. To make a cow take a bull

It is sometimes necessary to promote this desire in cows as otherwise the most profitable time for making butter or cheese might be lost. It is much better when nature is permitted to perform her own office, but this cannot always be dispensed with.

I did not offer you the special milk
smelling of aniseed and mixed

with grains of paradise, cantharides
and bayberries, freshly powdered,

for it is best to leave it to nature;
and this cure was not designed for humans

who are more often found to be susceptible
to Pernod, blackcurrant and cider.

iv. How to extract a calf when it presents itself in a wrong position

It is well known to all who have management of cows, or those who practise medicine among them, that calves are very commonly presented in a variety of different postures, for which no just reason can be assigned. And whenever they present themselves in a wrong posture both cow and calf are in danger, and that more or less according to the ability of the person employed to give the necessary assistance.

Sometimes you know too much
so all those antenatal classes –
talks on breathing, relaxation
and back rubs – were for nothing.
The monitor linked up to you
revealing all the warning signs
a distressed weakening heartbeat
beneath your own still strong pulse.

The unhooking, the unlocking
the emptying of the room.
Your bed pushed out the door
racing on towards the theatre
clogs clattering down the corridor
leaving me behind in the silence:
a cord round our child's neck,
all of us struggling to breathe.

v. Proper treatment of cows that slink or slip their calves in an
early period of gestation

Cows are most likely to slink their calves towards the latter end
of the year, while feeding on fog, or autumnal grasses; or on low
marshy grounds; and at other times it has proceeded from the smell
of carrion which may have been exposed in the pasture, or too
lightly covered with earth.

We never knew the reason.
What difference would it make?
But we won't forget the date of loss.
Christmas Eve – the tree and tinsel
in the ward, carol singing on departure.
The opening and closing
of the automatic doors at reception
an empty embrace of nothing
but night's chill air.

vi. The Hoose

The hoose or cough proceeds from taking cold from being kept in
a warm hovel and afterwards exposed to the inclemency of the
weather.

Mother you had a cough for as long as I remember
and though you worked outside your whole life

through the worst of West of Scotland weather,
four seasons rain delivered year in year out,

it was the habit that you picked up from my father
and could not shift no matter how much you tried –

that lighting up, the small release from the day
that gave you the bark to punctuate your breaths.

So, taking a balsam of sulphur, barbadoes-tar
beating yolks of two eggs in a large basin

adding ginger, aniseeds, cumin seeds, liquorice root
carbonate of soda, even the small sweetness of honey

and mixing them together little by little to a gruel –
a foul drink taken with warm milk

no matter the measures used or how often,
not even the chemo of those last few months

would have made any difference to your hoose.

vii. Angle-berries

Throw the animal down and take hold of the angle-berry at the base
with a pair of broad flat barnacles (such as are used in farriery)
then take a firing iron, after it has been sufficiently heated, and sear
or burn it off; touch the seared part all over with a skewer dipped in
oil or vitriol.

Father, you saw little difference
in the symptoms and ills of the afflicted
whether they be beast or man
though clever doctors
would vary the language used
to describe it, evolving it over time;
the cures too changing their names.

An expert in animal husbandry
you knew what needed to be done
to ease suffering in all species
to make them valuable to the farm,
so eager to return to parlour and pasture
you would offer yourself up
time and again to the surgeon's knife.

viii. Locked jaw

A sudden stagnation of the whole system; every muscle seized at once, and the jaws are so fast closed.

I read it can be triggered by a wounding.
I do not doubt that, but I need my words
more than ever, willing to do what it takes.

I am in the middle of the winter season
so like the beasts bleed me up to five quarts
throw two or three pails of warm water over me.

Rub me down with a warm blanket
take two drachms of opium,
one ounce of asafoetida,

mix them together in a marble mortar,
gradually adding a pint of boiling water,
keep constantly stirring till all is dissolved;

then add aromatic spirit of ammonia,
ginger, in powder, one ounce; cayenne pepper;
four tablespoons of treacle.

Force my jaws apart
feed me twice a day this cure of warm gruel.
Give me back my voice.

Casting a Cow, Ringing a Bull

(found poem after R.W. Blowey)

i.

Because a crush is not always the best approach to take
when you want to correct a displaced abomasum in a cow
I would favour the Reuff's method with a small sedation.

First steady the cow with a halter, then tie a second rope
around her neck, looping it behind both her forelegs
before taking it in front of the udder, hind legs and pin bones.

Tighten the chest rope and pull hard on the free end
to close the abdominal loop. With sufficient tension
the sick animal will slowly tilt and sink to the ground.

ii.

This is best carried out on bulls of less than six months.
Hold the head firm, divide the nostril to apply a nose punch.

Make the hole far back in the nostrils for added strength
but not through the harder tissue of the cartilage.

Having firmly closed the punch move it up and down
to cut the hole completely through then insert the ring.

Carefully turn the screw into the thread, ensure it's tight.
Break off the protruding segment, file down any rough edges.

Allow a month of healing before training the bull to lead.

Four Millimetres

Three days after the injection of tuberculin –
avian at the upper site, bovine at the lower

the vet returns for a lesson in small margins.
She illustrates the distance of four millimetres

between her forefinger and her thumb
as the first animal is brought to the crush.

The two scissor-clipped sites on its neck
are measured with careful precision.

The difference in thickness of skin
caught between the calliper pincers

could lead this cow to isolation, slaughter
the rest of the herd trapped on the farm.

She records her measurements on a clip board,
rechecks her figures, takes a lifetime to speak.

Warning Signs

Each day and night we've walked the shed
checking for evidence of fever, a dullness
among the young and vulnerable
or a cough we've witnessed in the past
spreading like a slow-moving wave
from pen to pen, leaving small corpses
as crumpled sacks in its wake.
Painful lessons have been learned
and, old herdsman, you do not let me forget
that prevention is key for survival –
the timing and quality of colostrum
is vital; castration and disbudding
should be carried out away from weaning.
Any additional stresses reduce immunity
so limit transport in the first few weeks.
Avoid overcrowding – early separation
and isolation can save lives you reminded me
as, sweat drenched, you wrestled a calf.
Be wary of underlying conditions like scour.
Shelter the future herd from cold and wet.
Clean bedding – do not skimp on straw.
Fresh air at calf level but not a draught.
Avoid extremes – it is all about looking
for a perfect balance; one you tell me
that has been lost from this world.
Everything is connected – pigs, civets,
camels, bats. Again, your hoarse bark
interrupts your flow as you nod to the valley
where a city now shares the silence of the hill.
Don't ignore the small signs, before the big.

We've stretched and torn mother nature.
How often have you told me this;
your teaching almost inbred, a hefting.
Today I pay more attention to you,
the wheeze in your breath.

The Shepherd's Loss

Some deaths at lambing time
are just too hard to recall
with a simple two fingers to fate.

That night, there was no real choice:
a lamb too big for birth,
a mother ruptured, bleeding out.

On your own with blade sharpened
you sawed through skin, sinew and bone;
silenced a new life to save the old.

Your bloodied hands holding a severed skull
was if Goliath had won the struggle
and as a trophy taken David's head.

Robertson's First Wake

Robertson wanted to attend his own wake while still living.
His rationale clear – why would he want to miss out on time
drinking with old pals he'd probably be funding anyway.
So, the night came, and he was surrounded by his own guest list
crammed into the three small rooms of his croft and nobody
was surprised how few of his relations made the cut – family
feuds being a speciality of his – fewer presents to be forked out
come Christmas. Despite being told not to, his cousin Fraser
wore his funeral suit and tie, hovered all night in one corner,
a haunting for those present. Crawford, his neighbour, wrote
a speech focussing on his teenage years: harvests and dances.
Brogan offered up some verses he'd penned for the occasion
telling the journey of a mystical hare. Some whispered later
he'd read the very same poem at a wake the month before.
The rest of the night was taken over by laughter and the dram
like two lovers reunited arm in arm walking through the past.
Robertson at the heart with an oxygen cylinder as his plus one,
content to listen to the talk of old men as hours flew by.
Only once was the spell broken when a sudden hush spread
among those there and an absence harrowed that silence.
Dawn scattered the remnants of the party out into the soil
of a new day, leaving the host already asleep in his chair,
the only one who would make his second wake.

MacIntyre's Big Horse

When the horse died, we all brought a shovel
joined Mac at the back of the paddock
to dig the grave and relive her life.

And we did so for hours, it was not a burden
for she was without doubt a great horse.
We watched again as she grew from foal

to yearling, to a mare eighteen hands high.
We recalled each field she had ploughed
the shows she won, the offspring she bore.

Completing our labours in the dark
we were glad to walk her journey again
with Mac a willing guide, we all cried.

When Mac himself died a decade later
the service was led by a visiting priest
in a rush to be somewhere else. He used

Mac's Sunday name that nobody recognised
led us in hymns that nobody knew and
in five sentences read out a stranger's life.

At the cemetery Mac's only living relative
took time to shake hands with his lawyer.
They filled in his grave with a JCB.

Preparing the Ground
(i.m. Archibald Stewart 1929–2015)

A teenager walks the heavy horses' rhythm.
His whole world is of harness, rein, and plough.

With rare, sharp commands he's in control
setting out the direction of the journey.

Ahead lies the rough ground to be broken.
In his wake a straight furrow, frenzy of gulls.

Did he ever lift his cloth-capped head to gaze
beyond sweating horizons of Clydesdale and cob

allow his thoughts to turn to future seasons
or did he never waver from the task in hand

to finish this very field where seven decades later
his working life and body were laid to rest?

Migration

Those days your eyes were darting swifts
under the rafters, alert to possibilities
but here in the same byre that look is lost;
this long winter has frozen your stare.
You blow into your fingers for warmth
scarred hands cupped like an empty nest.

Gone Out

Robert Carruth (1937–2013)

September nights from my youth
when you'd half finish your tea
rush back out to the cows on the hill
to monitor the pregnant mothers
make sure you were there to safeguard
each calf's first few minutes on Earth.

And though I pleaded to go with you
mother would tell me it was too late
struggling with my tantrums and tears.
Not brave enough to say no to my face
you would just sneak out the back door
slip your boots on, whisper to the collies.

Today I arrive at your hospital bed.
Silent, weak, you will never waken.
Without a goodbye you leave me again.
Somewhere beyond the cries of loved ones
you're walking your dogs in that far field
watching the herd, waiting for the next life.

My Father's Soil
(24 December 2013)

Christmas Eve, and at our doorstep
a basket of Golden Wonders newly dug
by my brother who lifted them alone
bending tear-blind into a bitter wind
as it strengthened all day to a storm.

These are taken from my father's soil –
he, who nurtured each from seed,
put in hard hours through the seasons
till they were fully grown and ready to eat.
For years we have received his harvest

left hanging on the door, bags heaving
with cabbages, carrots, wrist-thick leeks
the flowering of a vegetable bouquet.
There can be no better feast in life
than the gifts that only loved ones bring.

Tomorrow, he won't be at our table
surrounded by the fruits of all his labours
to lay out his beloved mash and roast
watching our sad longing devour it all:
his love for us, his loss, his final crop.

STEPPING STONES

Defiant and thrawn
Autumn's last leaf holding on
All the others gone

Stepping Stones

I have not paused mid-stream before
to consider all the effort put in
to build this crossing over the Locher.

The finding, the lifting, the laying
the testing of the next step, out and back
growing the journey across the water.

Some stones will have disappeared
dropped in places too deep for sight
a foundation for those that follow

while others, refusing to remain steady,
dislodged too easily by the burden of a foot,
have been carefully removed and replaced.

Since that day the work was finished
this route has been my way, confident
in the builder and their creation –

the journey of dry feet from bank to bank.
This trust has skipped across their line at night
taking on the white water of a river in spate.

The Course of the Locher Water

The narrow burn skirts the edge of our land.
Cattle drink from it at the bottom of three fields.

I rarely follow its course from the deep pool,
the tight bend, steep bank, its heartbeat

meander across the meadow land and under
the old stone bridge, before losing itself

in the cover of overhanging willow and oak.
When I do, I always stop at the border

of our farm, accept the rest of its journey
as a given: content to take in faith

the story of its source as a slow seep
and gargle in a bog high on the moor;

can picture it clear in my mind
without the need to have seen it surface

and trust too in the accuracy of maps
how downstream it is a river then ocean.

Today, standing here at our boundary fence.
I hold firm to my belief in moss and salt.

Traveller

So, you are seriously telling me
you've never had a passport?

Incredulity rising in the voice
of the door-to-door salesman

was always meant to wound
the eighty-nine-year-old farmer

who had struggled off his chair
to answer the bell and endure this

put down - simply a precursor
to a litany of foreign destinations

rattled off at speed like conquests;
but why belittle this man

who understands all that's required
to fully reap journey's harvest

learning that comes from travelling
the paths of seasons and years

who knows it's about taking your time
as he does before his answer:

Shuir whit wad A need ane o yon fur? –
A dinnae ken weel eneuch yet ma ain brae.

Old Boots

Found in ankle-length wet fescue
in the centre of the field by the wood.

Not dropped from a height or discarded
in a rush but carefully placed side by side

lying comfortably together as old lovers do
with the best of their years behind them.

There was no one around but the wind
shaking conversations from the trees;

no clues either to arrival or departure
in comet tails of bent and flattened grass.

I reached down to pick them up
not understanding this sign or gift.

Hard worked for sure – countless seasons
where roads were often the last resort.

It was clear the laces didn't match –
the black one on the left a recent addition.

A couple of metal eyelets were missing.
Turning them over – soles not yet worn through,

one heel's steep slope hinted at hirple or limp.
I placed my hands inside them – they were dry.

I traced the stitching on the welt
touched the rough edge of toe cap,

a barley grain caught on the tongue –
small clues of their journey

as was the smell of the faded leather I held
conch-like to my ear listening for a life's echo.

Without an Epiphany from the Belly of a Whale

Without an epiphany from the belly of a whale
it took him much longer to return to his calling,
simply reappeared one day at the byre door.
True repentance is not a one-off utterance,
some far-from-heartfelt apology mumbled
with a back turned, a rough engine running

but found in the slow healing of a dirty wound
opening and closing as each tense hour unfolds
between two men who worked the beasts again.
Almost silent, these coarse-spoken hill partners
ploughed and seeded rough ground for harvest
the days of wandering over, a journey still to go.

Market Talk

Ringside, countrymen huddle close, rubbing, touching,
their words are a stone thrown in a muddied puddle.
I listen for a ripple but cannot break the tweed coven –
unwritten bond, mingled scent of hard work and beasts.

I'm left to glean for scattered grain at the field edge
pick up a grunt that stands for a paragraph, the next
a decade and a death, inching closer to place my ear
a cuckoo fledgling in their nest – greedy to be fed.

This common ground is leaching nutrients from soil
in never-ending rains *Drive shaft, udder clap* and *draft*.
Raw bitter laughter, conversation sweated through pores
and I, the willing stranger, trying to keep it all safe,
savour swear-word flavoured *Slurry, stirk* and *straw*.

With a crossbill's twisted beak, I'm desperate to unpick
prise open, release the seed of meaning inside each cone
before the auctioneer's staccato chatter silences their talk.

Long Way Round

Instead of going straight home from the market
Lawson found time in his day to wander off

down country lanes past all his neighbours
peeping his horn, parading his recent purchases

bleating behind him, jammed in his small float.
He had paid a record price for these sheep –

a French breed with an unpronounceable name
never seen before in the fields of the district.

We had to stand in the ditch to let them through
returned his wave, noting first the fine thin wool

then the shivers rippling through the new flock.
Clambering onto the road we watched them go.

Crawford's caustic comment spoke our thoughts
A long way round to digging your own grave.

Viewpoint

Later the two ageing cattlemen
will rest from their day's journey
lean against a five-barred gate
let a couple of hours pass them by.

At times they'll pause their talk
watch the wide tractor plough
a trail of gulls across field and sky
writing its story away from them

or lift their gaze to the moor –
the farmer by his off-road trike
shouldering bags of extra nutrients
to feed the hunger of his flock.

But mostly they'll just look back
at that great herd of all their days
gathering slowly at the gateway
patient, ready to be milked again.

Bringing in the Cows

There are days when you come to fetch them
and they are nowhere to be seen.
The brae empty of cattle offers a blank face.

Your hope is that they stand somewhere
beyond the rise of the field
where it stretches down to reach the marsh.

You send the collie up and over the ridge
so he too disappears from view
and you are left with nothing to bring home.

More and more urgent each command given
to send the working dog right and left
and away back across a field out of sight.

Though you whistle or shout until hoarse
the hill offers not one word back
no bark or bellow and all seems lost.

You are searching for what you cannot see
seeking the return of that
which might already have disappeared.

You long for one strong thick head
rising above the crest
a signal for the rush of the herd to come.

Corute

My Wife's Whistle

This whistle of yours is an elusive art
the rest of our family have failed to master.
The way you blow on two fingers trapped
between lips works collies on the flock
fields away on the hill above Wellees.

This call you also used on our children
in crowded shops, long western beaches
or later lost as adults in raucous rugby crowds,
was not what stopped me short, turned me back
to come to heel, to stay, at first, now, always.

My Brother's Cloud

This low-lying cumulus
circling the farm with its shadow
is here because in the last few years

you didn't take a gun to the heart of its dance,
chase it away but fed it instead: that careful spilling
at the edge of troughs, until now it's a thousand voices.

It does not threaten rain nor is a sign of anything
other than acceptance, so I catch you looking up
in your all-too-full days to lose yourself

in its endless shape shifting
in its heartbeat fluttering
lustre of murmuration

as you spiral, swoop,
drop, perch, rest,
alight.

My Father's Hands

i. Hold

He stretched his arms   as wide as he could   to embrace this land
and in time   the earth held him   as close as kin

ii. Recapturing the Bull

It happened more than once –
a bull rubbing old hair off its neck
till it slips loose from rusted chains
untethering itself from the stall.

Release brought a deep bellowed rage
bursting its banks to flood the farm
rising to fill the nightmares of a child.
You'd shout *Come* and I'd run to you

to be raised onto your shoulders
as you rescued me from this deluge;
placing me onto a shed's flat roof
before turning to take on the bull.

Rampaging through the passage
it shook the timbers beneath my feet
emerged blinking into the sunlit yard.
With you in its sights, it briefly paused

to tilt its strong skull, deadly horns
to stretch its neck, reclaim the sky.
You were waiting, ready for the attack
a knight, your lance – a pole and hook

to reach and clip the ring at the charge
hold on tight, calm the torrent of its fight.
I could never replicate your firm steer
stilling the waters of three heart beats.

iii. Tossing the Sheaf

To take a solid stance, a firm grip
both hands on the pitchfork
and hurl a burlap bag of sixteen pounds

stuffed with straw above your head
and over the bar is a skill honed
in hours under the hot sun of harvest.

Odd then to picture these country youths
competing indoors in the city
on a Saturday night at the Kelvin Hall.

In this event, my father overcame
the height and barn door physique
of others by technique alone.

A jazz fan – Benny Goodman's big band
he transposed their beat rhythm
both for the dancing and this

to perfect the timing of swing and lift
the sack soaring over the bar –
a pole vaulter released from their pole.

These nights were his brief escape
from the shackles of the land,
that raising up and letting go.

To stand by him was to follow his gaze
from his farmer's arms and hands,
the launch pad of shaft and prongs,

through the flight of a hessian sputnik
towards girders, roof beams, streetlights
the clear rural sky beyond.

iv. Bird Box

It was to be his birthday surprise for our youngest
so my father sneaked into the garden in our absence.

One neighbour spotted him, with his replacement knee
and hip clambering onto a wheelie bin shoogling

as he swung a mell above his head knocking the stab
straight in the ground with the bird box facing north.

Everything had to be right he told us when we got back:
the height above the ground away from the predators;

the size of hole for small birds only; the depth of box
to protect the young. How he loved to watch them grow.

It was too new he said, needed to age a bit in the seasons
lose the human scent, so was unlikely to attract families

in the first few Springs. This year – eleven years after
he put it in the ground, four years after his own passing

they came for the first time, and we were entranced
as he knew we would be. The countless flights of blue tits

to first make a nest and then to feed the hungry young
the way his grandchildren ran back and forth to him

while he rested, age-weathered, in his big chair.

Gene Pool

You look just like your dad
is almost the first thing
the geneticist tells me
as I sit down in front of her
   and he was a lovely man

but his heart was too large.
In a missed heartbeat or two
she shuts down the sentimental
explaining simply the working
of this most complicated muscle

and what it's like for a normal heart
pumping blood to body and lungs.
I follow her finger and the flow
from atrium to ventricle and out
first on the right then the left;

how it is set out in regular rhythm
controlled by electrical impulses.
She turns to talk about relationships
the curse of dilated cardiomyopathy
connecting DNA to heart failure.

On her screen is our family tree
my father's name circled among others
the hit and miss of genetic inheritance
those 50/50 odds of offspring receiving
an unwanted gift from their parent.

Atrial Fibrillation

is a wren's wingbeat trapped against the glass.
It's a moth flutter at the danger of a bare bulb.
It's in the gust of leaf rustle, a churn and drop
of racing burn; the flu shiver in a sickly lamb.

It's in the stumble of a calf's first steps
a heifer's bellow and stampede to new grass
an old cow's milk-fevered stagger and collapse
rushing, uncontrollable, fleeting.

Roe

I wasn't tracking, rather
saw you by chance in the clearing

but I love fresh snowfall in the forest
following the journeys of others –

refugees from the chill northerlies
foraging for grass, leaves, berries.

Between the trees the first flash of white
a heart shaped rump, tense lithe body of doe.

You raise your head skywards
black nose, large ears alert to clues.

Winter has taken away your gold-red coat
left you dull brown, short hair rippled by ribs.

Now fully grown how small your kind remain.
A short life too – first spotted a few years ago,

a sleeping fawn leaning on your mother,
you will not see out ten years in this wood.

Soon I'll walk here with your absence
but what does that mean for us today?

One of us is too frightened to move
for what they sense but cannot see

the other scared to breathe for fear
of losing what they have right now.

Aeolian Harp

(after Jean Giono)

Shepherds, on my death let me be
an Aeolian harp. Yoke my corpse,
unclothed, from two high pines;
string this lyre from tip to trunk.
From what is left of flesh and bone,
tighten each line ready for the tune
then go and tend your flocks
for this is still about the living.
Let the seasons shape me
the winds breathe on me,
the sky stream through me.
Let my voice not be my own.

Preparing the Pipe

By now all this is ritual,
the memory winter –
that scraping of the spent
from his pipe.
In living room's low light
his small penknife
emits a sliver of gleam –
wave crest across its rust.

The upturned bowl displays
its own ebony ebbtide shine
as he dunts on the grate
yesterday's remains.

Unrushed, his sprinkling touch
of tobacco into the bowl,
brings a careless lapping over
the side, softening the day.
One thumb gently compresses
the flakes till the hollow is filled.

His mantra of making do is seen
in the broken shank held to the stem
with an old worn piece of rubber
sliced from a milking machine.

He places the pipe on the table
delays the match flare and first draw
the haze that will surround him
and us in an evening of puffs
and tamping down of ashes.
Instead, he looks up and stares
through me, as though standing
at the edge of an ocean.

Vespers

There is a weariness
that comes on late in the day –
age is a grain sack
on your shoulders

your knees recalling
every mile walked –
so, you simply stop,
chant soft and slow

a litany of tasks
now left for tomorrow
then surrender completely
to your surroundings.

Let the senses escape
the grip of body and mind
finding there is still bird song
in the hedgerow

not the bring-it-on chorus
of many voices
but signoffs to the light
sporadic and muted.

As working day's colours
weaken into night
you pick up a barley grain
rub it without thinking

between fingers and thumb –
a deep breath
can still resurrect
the remnants of harvest

and through a little shiver
the season is changed.
a silent prayer
sprouts like a new shoot.

Milk Fever

The cow has quickly gone from a stiff walk
to lying flat out on her side in the cubicle stall
surrounded by the herd in the semi-darkness.

My father and I try to get her to sit upright
putting our backs into it with little success.
She has a shiver; I check, and her ears are cold.

I'm sent to the medicine cabinet by the bulk tank
bring back calcium, a clean needle and tubing
a bucket of warm water to take the chill off it.

He swiftly slips the needle under the skin
tells me to give the cow the best chance
I must keep the bottle up until the last drop.

Though my arms began to ache I did not let go.
Of all those in the shed that night only I survive
holding an empty brown bottle high like a beacon.

Planting Aspen Saplings

Planting aspen saplings
father and son

though I might not live to see
them grow to full height

their grey bark covered in lichen
flowering catkins in the spring,

or listen to their leaves tremble
at the slightest breeze.

Son, you're quick to share
the story of this native's decline

how this is where it belongs –
a wet moorland on the west.

You talk of the nature of roots
the unseen suckers underneath

how colonies from a single seed
can endure a thousand years

even sending up new trunks
in a forest fire's charred aftermath.

You tell me of the tree's offer
to gall midges, birds, hare, deer

the importance of relationships
the interconnectedness of everything.

They do not thrive in shade, need light
and space to grow.

Planting aspen saplings,
son and father.

ACKNOWLEDGEMENTS

I would like to thank everyone who helped shape this collection, including Gerrie Fellows, Vicki Husband, William Bonar and John Glenday. I would also like to thank Edward Crossan and Polygon for their support of this book and the others.

I would also like to thank the editors of the following publications, where versions of some of the poems first appeared: the anthologies, *Antlers of Water*, *The Hunterian Poems*, *Postcards from Malthusia*, *New Writing Scotland* 35, 36, and papers and magazines, *The Causeway Magazine*, *The Dark Horse*, *Gutter*, *Herald*, *Long Poem* magazine.

'Earthstruck' was chosen by the Scottish Poetry Library as one of the twenty best Scottish poems of 2021.

'Planting Aspen Saplings' was recorded for the Scottish Poetry Library as part of the National Poetry day theme of 'Nature' in 2022.

'Market Talk' was part of the Year of Conversation online project curated by Tom Pow.

'Viewpoint' was first published in *The Wicca Woman* – a celebration of Betty McKellar's ninetieth birthday.

'My Father's Soil' was commissioned to be part of *Christmas Stories: Twelve Poems to Tell and Share* published by Candlestick Press

The BBC created a video of a version of 'Shearing' as part of my time as poet in residence at The Royal Highland Show.